MW00902023

How to Write a Letter

By Scribendi.com

Print Edition

ISBN: 1492269093
ISBN-13: 978-1492269090

CONTENTS

SCRIBENDI

INTRODUCTION TO LETTER WRITING

What do you think when you hear the word "letter"?

Merriam-Webster (2013) defines a "letter" as "a direct or personal written or printed message addressed to a person or organization." It's a means of communicating something to someone else, and until the invention of Morse's telegraph in the nineteenth century, it was the only way of doing so over long distances. But what does a letter mean to us *today*?

Letter writing is not something we consider as needing to be learned; it's just a task we all feel we know how to do. Think about it: you know that you should start a letter with "Dear so and so," and end it with a closing line like, "Yours sincerely" or "With love." When you stop and reflect, however, these are conventions you had to be taught.

Letter writing has to be taught because it is a specific kind of writing. Just as you would follow guidelines when composing an essay or a poem, which are both distinctive *kinds* of writing, rules and structural requirements must be followed in order to write a successful letter. There is no single set of guidelines, either; of the many different kinds of letters, each has its own purpose and requirements.

Unfortunately, letter writing is somewhat of a lost art. Though the basics may still be taught in schools, they are easily forgotten in our world of texting, e-mails, and instant messaging. It's much easier to tap out a quick e-mail or make a phone call now that we're connected worldwide, and it costs next to nothing to get in touch.

Despite the convenience of instant communication, letters are still essential in today's world. Therefore, this guide is designed to help you recognize what a particular situation calls for, whether a handwritten letter or a typed e-mail would present the best approach, how to structure your letter's content, and how to ensure your intended result. Knowing how to write an effective correspondence isn't limited to pen and paper; the skills you develop through letter writing are transferrable to other mediums, like e-mails, texts, memos, faxes, and so on.

Letters once provided the only means for people to communicate over a significant distance. As Malcolm Jones (2009) put it, "modern communication technologies have slowly but all too surely eroded that necessity, first rendering letter-writing one option among many and then merely a quaint habit." The obsolete state of letter writing in today's fast-paced world is a cause for concern, as those who have grown up completely accustomed to and comfortable with digital communications, such as texting and e-mail, may never actually put their basic letter-writing skills to use.

However, knowing how to write a successful letter is just as essential now as it has ever been. It doesn't matter whether you're applying for a job, thanking a relative for a Christmas present, or apologizing to a customer for a service error. Each of these situations can be handled with an appropriate letter. A letter is the most basic—yet the most flexible—mode of correspondence, regardless of its subject matter.

Some forms of letters have proven more resilient than others, and they're still quite common in everyday situations. The examples of letters outlined in this book attest to this fact, and although most of them are typically written electronically, the letters themselves are important for giving and receiving information.

Think about the last letter you received. It may have been a handwritten missive from a friend or relative, or a pre-printed card with only a salutation and signature scrawled on it. Perhaps it was an official-looking business correspondence or a sales letter wanting you to buy something or sign up for a new credit card. Maybe it was even junk mail that you immediately threw in the trash. Now, consider the purpose of that letter. Was it to inform, persuade, complain, or perhaps just to connect? Did it succeed?

That is exactly what this guide will teach you: how to write effective letters that will achieve their desired aims, while keeping the art of letter writing alive.

Are you ready to learn the art of letter writing?

PART ONE: MEDIUM AND METHOD

To appreciate letter writing today, we must acknowledge the modern contexts in which letters need to be written. While traditional handwritten letters should not be overlooked, they are not suitable for most circumstances. Similarly, mailing letters is not always practical if a quick dispatch is required; this is where e-mail comes in. Becoming an effective letter writer means analyzing each situation individually and choosing the form of correspondence accordingly.

Handwritten letters versus typed letters

Think about those occasions where it *is* common practice to write by hand. We still do so with greeting cards, even if they have pre-printed messages inside. Greeting cards are intended to convey an emotion, be it our best wishes, congratulations, thanks, or condolences. Postcards are also handwritten, sent from a vacation spot somewhere to let the recipients know they are missed.

This is the perfect use for a handwritten letter—to express a sentiment and closeness to the recipient. Handwriting takes more time than typing and requires greater care and attention. Sending a handwritten letter shows that you are happy to invest extra effort into your communication and demonstrates how much the recipient means to you.

The following are the *benefits* of a *handwritten letter*:

1. Adds a personal touch and communicates emotion
2. Looks more appealing than print, if written well
3. Can be made more interesting and eye-catching with specialized stationery and pens
4. Shows the recipient you have spent time and effort on the letter itself

On the other hand, here are some *disadvantages*:

1. Takes longer to write than a typed letter
2. May not look presentable or legible if one's penmanship needs improvement (though this is even more reason to keep practicing!)
3. More difficult to fix mistakes

Handwritten letters should *not be used* in the following cases:

1. When you are writing a formal or business correspondence rather than a personal one
2. When you are addressing someone you don't know
3. When you don't have much time and need to quickly communicate with the recipient

Of course, there are exceptions to these guidelines, and it's important to recognize when a situation calls for a more appropriate rule. For example, in terms of the first rule in the preceding paragraph, you wouldn't handwrite a job application letter, as the hiring manager would expect a cover letter and résumé to be typed and sent electronically.

A letter can be typed using word processing software like Microsoft Word or Apple's iWork Pages. It can then be printed and mailed or sent as an e-mail attachment. You can also type your message directly in an e-mail, but make sure to follow the submission requirements for a document like a cover letter or a résumé, as these often need to be attached individually, and sometimes in a specified format.

The downside is that typed letters can be quite impersonal. In other words, they are appropriate for formal situations, but not for communicating with close friends or family. To circumvent this unintended effect, such as in invitations and newsletters, you can leave a blank space where the greeting and signature are meant to be, and insert the recipient's name and sign your name by hand. However, please note that e-mail service platforms also feature a personalized option to customize mass mailings (addressing each recipient by name and adding the sender's electronic signature). You can even take this a step further and leave space for a personalized sentence or two.

Finally, a typed letter has a more formal and professional appearance than a handwritten version. Both employers and customers expect business communications to come in typed form. In such instances, handwriting is considered unprofessional since it can be difficult to read; therefore, if you send a handwritten correspondence, you risk your letter being thrown away by the recipient.

Now, let's look over the *advantages* of a *typed letter*:

1. Takes less time than handwriting
2. Can be sent either electronically or in the mail
3. Can be repeatedly rewritten, with the advantage of spelling and grammar checks
4. Appears more formal and professional than a handwritten letter
5. Multiple copies of the same letter can be sent to different people
6. Can be saved on your computer for future reference

However, the *disadvantages* of typed letters are as follows:

1. Can look impersonal and distance the recipient from the sender
2. Can encourage you to quickly type out a letter without really thinking about what you're writing
3. Can look dull and boring, with only limited customization available

For these reasons, *typed letters* are *most appropriate* in the following circumstances:

1. When you are writing to someone you don't know and want to keep things professional
2. When you need to send the same letter to multiple recipients
3. You need to produce and send a letter as quickly as possible

Physical letters versus digital letters

There are still some situations, however, in which a physical letter is most suitable.

We need to remember the power of a physical object that can be held or touched. Letters that people can see in front of them have a unique force. J.K. Rowling's *Harry Potter and the Sorcerer's Stone* gives us an excellent example: Why does Harry receive a *letter* inviting him to Hogwarts rather than an e-mail, a phone call, or even a telepathic message transmitted straight into his mind? Because if he did, we wouldn't have the brilliant images of those letters pouring down the chimney, popping out of the toaster, and forcing their way through the nailed-shut mailbox! It is their physical presence that drives Uncle Vernon so mad.

The physicality of a letter is something completely lost in digital communications. Receiving a letter becomes a process of anticipation; the letter has to be picked up, held, opened, removed from its envelope, and perhaps unfolded before it can be read. Double clicking an e-mail attachment isn't half as much fun.

A physical letter is also special because it is something you can keep. It leaves a legacy in a way that digital communications, deletable with a mouse click, cannot. This makes physical letters valuable souvenirs— reminders of times and people past. On a less sentimental note, physical letters can be retained for evidence of sale, proof of address, or other practical purposes, as there are times when you may need such documents on record.

Now, let's quickly recap the *advantages* of sending a *physical letter*:

1. The physicality of a letter lends it a certain power, making it difficult to ignore.
2. Tangible letters can be kept and reread, either for sentimental or business purposes.
3. Sending a physical letter shows that you have put time, effort, and even money into your communication.

Of course, there are also some *downsides*:

1. Sending a letter in the mail takes time and costs money.
2. Physical letters can be lost or damaged, while a digital copy is safe from physical harm. (Note: Digital files can be corrupted, "lost," or difficult to retrieve/restore without a backup copy.)
3. A physical letter requires additional material before it can be sent (i.e., an envelope and a stamp).

So, the most *appropriate situations* for sending a *physical letter* are as follows:

1. When the contents of the letter are meaningful or valuable enough that you want the recipient to keep the hard copy
2. When you want to send a strong message, be it emotional, professional, or political
3. When the letter does not need to arrive instantly

Remember that every case is different and should be evaluated independently to make sure you are taking the right steps. For example, if you are trying to contact an individual whom you know is traveling around with no fixed address, an e-mail is obviously a more appropriate medium of communication.

Sending an e-mail is instant, now more so than ever. In the past, though an e-mail might have arrived immediately, it would only be read when the recipient checked his or her messages on a computer. Now, with e-mails being frequently downloaded to our smartphones, tablets, and other portable devices, instant really *means* instant. The reverse is also true; we can send messages in seconds and from anywhere, as long as we have an Internet connection.

When you know your message will arrive promptly, you are able to submit it with plenty of time to spare, or if you're struggling, you can continue working right up to the deadline. You can guarantee your message will be received on time, and you can prove it, if necessary, with the automatic time stamp on every e-mail saved in your Sent Items folder.

It's important to be able to recognize when an e-mail fits a situation. In the past, e-mails were considered suitable only for casual communication, but today, e-mail can be used for a wide variety of situations, including more formal exchanges. For instance, communicating with co-workers via e-mail is now general practice—but make sure you keep things professional and in accordance with workplace policies. Knowing how to write different kinds of e-mails is just as important as knowing how to write different kinds of letters.

Let's review the *advantages* of sending a letter electronically, either in an *e-mail* or as an *e-mail attachment*:

1. Arrives instantly and can be read straight away
2. Can be sent from and accessed anywhere with an Internet connection
3. Doesn't cost anything
4. Is now considered appropriate for a broad range of situations

It's also important to remember the *disadvantages*:

1. An e-mail can be misdirected or end up in a Junk Mail folder, where it won't be read.
2. An e-mail can be easily deleted, either intentionally or unintentionally.

3. Confidentiality issues may arise if the recipient forwards the message to others.
4. Some situations still require a physical copy of your letter, and e-mail submissions may be ignored.

So, the most *appropriate situations* for sending your *e-mail* in digital form are as follows:

1. When your message should reach the recipient as soon as possible
2. When you need to attach multiple documents or images, which takes time and money to print and send physically
3. When you need to send a message while you're out and about

Since most people and businesses have their own e-mail addresses, they are that much more open to receiving digital communication. Remember that even though an e-mail is the easiest way to send a letter, it isn't always the best method, especially if you're trying to convey a personal, meaningful message.

PART TWO: DIGITAL COMMUNICATION

You can do many things with word processing software, such as Microsoft Word, Apple's iWork Pages, or Open Office Writer, from changing the font to adding page borders and images. To start, you only need to know the basics, and changing the font of your document is as simple as it gets. In the interest of readability, it's best to stick with a clear font, like Times New Roman, Calibri, or Arial. The default size is 12 points, though if you choose to work with a small or large font, you'll need to adjust the size accordingly. If you do decide to experiment with more interesting fonts, limit them to personal correspondence. Keep your business letters just that—strictly business!

Some basic standards act as guidelines when word processing any document, like the fonts and font sizes just mentioned. Here are a few others to bear in mind.

Margins: Flush left, ragged right margins are considered the standard for most word processed documents.

Spacing: Around 1.5 line spacing keeps your documents readable without adding too much white space.

Font effects: Keep bold, italicized, and underlined text to a minimum. Use these effects only when necessary and ensure consistency. For example, if you use italics for emphasis, *always* use italics; don't switch between italics and bold or underline.

If typing a particular type of correspondence, such as a cover letter for a certain company, check whether the company requires any formatting specifications.

One of the biggest mistakes writers make is becoming complacently dependent on spelling and grammar checks. Some mistakes can creep through these filters and leave you looking silly or careless if you don't proofread the document yourself. Homophones, for example, can be easily missed. The following sentences illustrate how easy it is to make a spelling error:

- I found it over their. **(there)**
- I can't bare this any moor. **(bear, more)**
- I've bean this way since birth. **(been)**

For more examples of these kinds of situations, please see Scribendi.com's frequently mixed-up words index.

See how easily embarrassing mistakes can slip under the radar? That's why you should always proofread your letters, even if the spell check isn't showing any errors.

One final note about word processors is to always take advantage of the Print Preview function. This allows you to view your full document, one or several pages at a time, to see how it will look when printed. Checking the preview before printing your document often saves you having to edit and reprint it, thus simultaneously saving you time and additional printing costs.

Professionalism

E-mails must be well written and appropriate to the context in which they are being sent in order to successfully achieve their purpose. The approach to writing an e-mail should be the same as writing a letter, and you should treat them both with an equal level of planning and forethought.

Ensure you're sending your e-mail to the right address—not just correctly typed, but also to the appropriate recipient. If you're trying to reach someone about a business matter and that person has a business e-mail address, he or she could be irritated to receive your message at a personal address. The reverse situation could also be a problem. Try to keep personal communication on an appropriate forum, or you or your recipient could get in trouble for misusing a work e-mail account.

Likewise, you should carefully manage your own e-mail addresses. Many people maintain multiple e-mail accounts; for example, one for personal use and one for work, similar to keeping two cell phones. You may wish to create your own professional address or your employer may give you one on the corporate server. In the latter case, the address will almost certainly be simple and professional—something you should emulate when creating your own. It doesn't look impressive if you're e-mailing your résumé from a personal address that's something like "cutiepie1990@hotmail.com."

To attach a file to your e-mail, be it a document, image, audio file, etc., it's best to name the file something obvious that indicates its contents, for example:

- MartinJamesResume.docx
- jennysbirthdaycake.jpg
- Fun-WeAreYoung.mp3

This ensures that the recipient can identify what's in the file, as people can (sensibly) be quite suspicious of strange attachments that could potentially carry viruses. For this reason, you should also state clearly in the body of your e-mail what you have attached and why. Here are some suggestions:

- I am interested in the position of Sales Assistant at your store and have attached my résumé for your consideration.
- The cake was incredible! I've attached a picture so you can see for yourself.
- Attached is the song that Debbie asked to have played at the staff party. Could you please add it to the playlist?

Finally, before attaching a file to an e-mail, try to find out in what format the recipient would prefer to receive it. For documents, Microsoft Word files are most commonly used, though a company asking for your résumé may specify PDF or another format; it is extremely important to pick up on this information. Similarly, consider the attachment's size. If you're sending a picture to someone whom you know will retrieve it on his or her cell phone, scale down a huge image file that will otherwise take ages to download.

Above all, make sure your e-mail is readable and courteous:

- Ensure proper and consistent spacing.
- Avoid distracting fonts and inconsistent font styles, sizes, colors, or formats.
- Write a clear and concise subject line; your e-mail should follow suit.
- Name your attachments properly and check that they are appropriately sized (not too big or too small).

PART THREE: PREPARING, PLANNING, AND STRUCTURING YOUR LETTER

Purpose and goals

To begin, think about the purpose of your letter. Ask yourself the following questions: To *whom* am I writing? *What* am I writing about? *Where* is this letter going? *When* should I send it? *Why* am I writing it? *How* much information does the recipient already know about me? *How* formal should I be? Do I know the recipient personally? To help avoid ambiguity, try your best to anticipate the questions your letter might raise and answer them through its content.

You will also want to establish a context for your letter by providing adequate information on the **five Ws and one H** mentioned above: *who, what, where, when, why,* and *how.* Answering these questions will build the foundation of your letter and will allow you to write clearly and confidently. Refer to the examples below. Think about how you would answer the questions in each situation:

Situation 1 – Job Loss: Who lost his or her job? Were other people (co-workers, family members) affected by this person's loss? What is this person going to do now? Did this person know he or she would be losing his or her job, or did it catch him or her off-guard?

Situation 2 – Invitation: What am I being invited to? When is it? When do I need to RSVP, and to whom should I direct my response?

Situation 3 – Work Project: When does the project need to be completed? To whom will this project be submitted?

Situation 4 – Congratulations: Why am I congratulating this person? Will this person be holding an event to celebrate?

Situation 5 – General Questions: Why am I writing this letter? To whom am I addressing it? What am I writing about? What is my relationship to this person? Where does this person live? What can I do to help this person? How formal should my writing be?

Once you're in the right disposition, with the tools and materials necessary to write your letter, you're ready for the preparation and planning process.

Preparation and planning

When preparing to write your letter, think about what you want to say and how you want to say it. What kind of mindset should you be in when writing? One of the major benefits of letter writing is that it allows you to think carefully about what you write without the risk of flaring emotions or mood swings. It's always best to write your letter in a calm and positive state of mind, even if the letter is a complaint or a note of sympathy. If you write your letter while angry, don't send it immediately. Reread it once you've had the chance to cool off and then think: Is this really the way I want to present myself? Is this letter really going to help me achieve my goals? How will its language or tone affect the recipient?

Sitting down to write a letter, regardless of whether it's business or personal, is like setting up for work. Like many writers, you may find it helpful to follow a bit of a routine to get you started. Here are a few ideas:

1. Eliminate all distractions to make sure you won't be disturbed while you write. Mute or turn off your phone, ask the family to

     give you some time to yourself, and make sure the television or computer doesn't make any annoying sounds. This will allow you to focus and write a cohesive, smooth-flowing letter.

2. Have a dedicated room or other quiet space where you go to write. This might be at home, a peaceful nook at the park, an undisturbed spot on campus, a coffee shop, or a table at the library.

3. Gather together all the relevant materials you may need to write the letter. For example, if you're responding to a letter, have it in front of you in case you need a quick review. If you're typing a status report for a project at work, make sure to have all the materials on hand. The last thing you want is to interrupt your task to go rifling through drawers or filing cabinets.

Planning is an essential part of any project, even something as seemingly simple as writing a letter. For brief letters, a plan shouldn't take more than a few minutes and can reduce the time you spend writing and editing. For longer and more complex letters, you may end up devoting more time on the plan than on the letter itself! In either case, if you want your letter to be successful, then you need to factor planning into the writing process.

Once you've identified your purpose and planned out your letter, you can draft a basic outline.

Outline

Your outline doesn't have to be extensive; its purpose is just to help you organize your thoughts and the material you will cover so that your letter will be as clear and cohesive as possible. Depending on the type and length of your letter, you can even jot down a few lines to help you start putting your thoughts on paper. Write down your main message or the points you want to make in the proper sequence, and also note any areas in which further research may be required (about a person, a company, a situation, etc.).

For example, if you're writing an application letter to a university for a master's program, you should know enough about the program and your reasons for pursuing it before putting pen to paper. You want to convey to your reader (in this case, an admissions officer) that you thoroughly understand the program and its structure, and that it's something you're both serious and passionate about.

Or, perhaps you are writing a condolence letter to a distant family member. In this case, you'll need to gather some background information about the person and his or her situation before your support and sympathy can shine through in your letter. Not only will this help you write a more sincere message; it will also express your general concern for the recipient.

You will want your outline to be structured chronologically so that your ideas are logical and easy to follow. Start with the four main sections of your letter:

1. Greeting
2. Introduction
3. Body
4. Sign-off

Greeting: Your greeting is a salutation that appropriately addresses the recipient.

Dear _____,

Dear Sir or Madam,

To whom it may concern,

Hi _____,

Hello,

My love,

John, (recipient's name)

Introduction: This section at the beginning of your letter allows you to make yourself known to the recipient. An introduction is necessary in a formal or professional letter or when writing to someone whom you do not know personally. Write a short paragraph telling the recipient about yourself and your reason for writing. This will establish a context for the reader and enable an appropriate response.

Body: The body of your letter comprises your main message; it is essentially your letter's content. It outlines (in greater detail than the introduction) the purpose of your letter (a thank you, a request, an acceptance, an invitation—the list goes on). The body may consist of one or a few paragraphs, depending on the length of your letter, and will contain the main points summarized in your outline, but in sentence form.

Sign-off: Just as your greeting is a salutation, your closing is a farewell. It should be appropriate to the recipient and the circumstance, and reflect a warm and personal or formal and cordial tone. Some examples are as follows:

- *Sincerely,*
- *Yours sincerely,*
- *Respectfully yours,*
- *Best,*
- *Kind regards,*
- *Yours truly,*
- *Love,*
- *With love,*
- *Best wishes,*
- *All the best,*
- *Cheers,*
- *Cordially,*
- *Thanks again,*
- *Take care,*
- *Your friend,*

Having completed the outline of your letter with a greeting, an introduction, a body, and a conclusion, you can now delve deeper into these areas by structuring your letter more tightly.

Structure

All letters, regardless of their type, follow the same general structure. After all, the structure of a letter gives it character and makes it stand out among all other forms of writing. Letters should be composed with the following structure (Stewart and Kowler 1991):

1. Your address and the date
   - o Place the address and the date in the upper right- or left-hand corner, single-spaced.
   - o If you are using letterhead stationery, write or type the date below the address, as your address will already be included within the letterhead.
2. Your recipient's address
   - o Place your recipient's address in the left margin, single-spaced.
   - o Include the same information you would put on the envelope.
3. The salutation, followed by a comma or a colon
   - o Use "Dear (name of person)" if you know to whom you are writing; if not, you may use "Dear Sir or Madam," or perhaps the particular position or company department you are addressing, such as "Dear Editor" or "Attention: Human Resources Department." Refer to the previous examples of greetings for more ideas.
4. The body of the letter
   - o This is where you will place the main message (or contents) of your letter. This section is composed of at least a couple paragraphs, even if they are short.
5. The complimentary closing
   - o Here, you may use a sign-off such as "Yours sincerely," "Sincerely," "Yours truly," "Kind regards," etc. Again, refer to the preceding examples of sign-offs for more ideas.

6. Your signature
   - You will then sign the letter by writing or typing your name or signature below the closing.
7. Enclosure(s)
   - If you will be including an additional document with your letter (a check, a résumé, a cover letter, a picture, or any other type of file), you may write "Enclosure" in the left margin, a couple of line spaces after your signature. For clarity, you may want to write "Check Enclosed" or "Résumé Enclosed," as the case may be.

Easy enough, right? Once you've carefully planned out the structure and outline of your letter, writing it will be effortless. In the next section, you will learn how to create your letter and explore the stylistic elements of tone and formality—two very important factors to keep in mind when writing any kind of letter.

PART FOUR: CREATING AN EFFECTIVE LETTER

After finishing the outline and structure of your letter, it's time to think about how to write it in greater depth. A variety of important factors affect the way in which you communicate your information, especially if you're requesting something from the recipient—which is often the reason for writing a letter. Let's take a closer look at a few of these elements.

To be effective, the letter you produce needs to be built around the needs, interests, and desires of your recipient. This is true of any kind of persuasive writing. The best way to get something from people and organizations is to demonstrate the benefit to *them*. Consider the following examples and the potential advantages to the recipients, should they grant what the letter asks:

- **A letter requesting the recipient to sign a petition:** The recipient will be part of a supporting community that will help a worthy cause, and the person's show of commitment will benefit his or her reputation.
- **A cover letter accompanying a résumé:** The recipient and the company will benefit from hiring the candidate, who will be a valuable addition to the team, helping achieve the company's goals.

- **A letter of complaint asking for a refund:** The business will increase the chances of the customer buying from it again if the matter is resolved to the customer's satisfaction. A positive response will enhance the company's reputation by reducing the risk of negative feedback.

Your letter needs to help the recipient recognize these rewards so that he or she will see a valid reason for acceding to your request.

In some letters, showing the recipient the positive impacts of granting your request may simultaneously involve highlighting the negative consequences, should the recipient decline the request. However, always tread cautiously! You don't want your recipient to feel as if he or she is being threatened or guilt-tripped into doing something, so be careful to phrase your text diplomatically and professionally. Compare the following pairs:

1. If you don't offer me a refund, then I will never shop here again, and I will tell all my friends not to shop here either! **versus** Unfortunately, if we cannot resolve this matter, I will be forced to take my business elsewhere, and will not hesitate to share my negative experience with others.
2. If you don't sign our petition, then you obviously don't care about helping starving children, and everyone will know it! **versus** Your signature on our petition would demonstrate your generous support of this cause, and it will be clear to your fans and peers that you care about the less fortunate
3. If you don't give me the job, you're missing out on a great opportunity, and it's your loss! **versus** I am confident that I will be a valuable asset to your team, and I believe that my skills and experience in this industry make me the right candidate for the position.

Appealing to your recipient and explaining the benefits to him or her is much easier if you know with whom you are dealing. The better you understand the recipient, the more effectively you will be able to communicate by targeting his or her wants and needs. Once you've done your research, if necessary, sit down with a pen and paper and ask yourself the following questions:

- **Who is going to read my letter?** Bear in mind that it may be more than just one person, as your recipient may pass the letter on.
- **What does this person already know about the subject?** While you want to ensure that your recipient is well informed, you will waste time by rehashing things that he or she already knows.
- **What else does this person need to know about the subject?** Make a list of the important points and think about how to best communicate them.
- **What is my relationship to the recipient?** This will affect the tone of your letter and the way in which you communicate the information and make your request.

Together, answering these questions will help you answer the most important one of all:

How can I effectively communicate my message in a way that the recipient will understand and agree with?

Answering this final question will help you write a successful letter that achieves its intended goal.

Tip: If you don't know the recipient personally, you may need to do some research. This doesn't mean stalking him or her, but there isn't any harm in a quick Google search. It's particularly important to find out the name of the person you're trying to contact; for example, if you're sending your résumé to the human resources (HR) manager at a particular company, browse the company's web site or call to ask for the HR manager's name so that you can address your letter correctly. This will make your communication more professional and less likely to be ignored than something addressed "To Whom It May Concern" or "Dear Sir or Madam." Don't worry too much if you can't find a name, but give it your best shot.

Tone and formality

Now that you've established the purpose and goals of your letter, and created an outline, it's time to focus on your tone and the level of formality. This will depend on two things: (1) the recipient (your audience) and (2) your purpose for writing the letter.

Tone refers to your expressiveness and is dictated by your audience and purpose. It is the manner in which you convey your emotions. A rule for setting the tone of your letter is to write how you would like the letter to read. If you are composing a cover letter, is it professional yet enthusiastic? If you are writing a condolence letter, is your tone sympathetic yet hopeful? Remember, you want your tone to reflect your audience, purpose, and feelings, but being upset or angry is no excuse for rude or vulgar writing.

Even if you're writing to discuss an unpleasant situation, try your best to maintain a civil tone throughout your letter. If possible, avoid writing a letter when you're in a bad mood; however, if you do write a letter while angry or upset, take some time to reread it once you've cooled down. You will most often realize that you have written things you didn't mean or didn't really want to say.

Ideally, write a letter when you are able to think clearly and rationally. If you do end up sending an ill-conceived letter or e-mail, apologize immediately either over the phone or in person, if possible. It is best to express your regrets sincerely and admit your mistake. To avoid getting into such a situation in the first place, first make sure that you're in the right state of mind to write your letter; then, in the case of sending an e-mail, wait until you're finished writing before filling in the "To" field. This is your best bet against (accidentally) sending something you didn't intend to or forwarding it to the wrong person. It will also give you a chance to review the content of your e-mail without impulsively hitting "Send." You will also want to avoid gossiping or talking negatively about others in your e-mails; e-mails are permanent and will forever be stored in a mail server. Besides, when all is said and done, it's just plain disrespectful to gossip about others—so avoid doing so at all costs!

Although the person you're writing to may be a close friend or family member, if your purpose is to discuss a business or professional matter, you should forego the conversational tone for a more formal approach. You can be friendly and familiar while still communicating in a professional manner. For example, if you're sending a wedding invitation, it's appropriate to be formal and cordial toward all your guests, *especially* family and friends. However, if you're writing a postcard to a close friend, your tone will be more conversational and natural.

The language you use should be clear and easy to understand. It should convey your tone, style, and voice. When writing an informal letter, you will more likely use slang, contractions, and colloquialisms. Your letter will resemble the way you would actually speak. When writing a more formal letter, you will want to avoid casual language and favor wording that is more complex, detailed, and respectful. By including facts, sensory details, definitions, quotations, or examples, you can tailor the content to your subject and change your voice accordingly to appeal specifically to your audience. This will allow you to be authoritative, make your writing more interesting, or even persuade the reader to believe your thoughts or ideas. In general, you should keep your language gender-neutral so as not to offend your audience. This is especially true when writing to someone whom you don't know personally or when you don't know whether the recipient is a man or a woman (when writing a cover letter to a hiring manager, for example). If you know the name of the person you are addressing, make sure to spell it correctly, as this is a sign of respect and will show your effort in finding out the recipient's identity.

If you're writing a letter to someone you have never met in person, such as a business contact or potential employer, your goal will be to create a favorable first impression. This will be revealed through your level of formality and your cordial yet sophisticated tone.

If you're writing an acceptance letter, ensure that it comes off as professional, but also enthusiastic about the opportunity. If you're writing a letter of congratulations, keep your tone light and cheerful.

Keeping these rules in mind will enhance your letter's effectiveness and produce an outcome that meets—or even exceeds—its purpose and goals.

PART FIVE: THE FIVE KEYS TO REALLY EFFECTIVE LETTERS

1. Brevity

The length of your letter will depend on its type and purpose. Generally, you should keep it brief—around one to two pages in length—if possible. You want your letter to be long enough to convey your information fully, yet not so wordy that it drags on with unnecessary details. A thank you letter, for example, will be short and straightforward, while a love letter will be expansive and much more vibrant and colorful in its phrasing. Try to keep your purpose in mind when considering the length (and thereby content) of your letter, and remember to keep things concise!

2. Specificity

Specificity goes back to purpose—what is the reason for writing your letter? Here, you will probably need to be explicit in answering the **five Ws and one H** (*who, what, where, when, why,* and *how*). Although you may not need to go into extensive detail, make sure that you provide *enough* information to get your point across clearly without confusing your recipient. Avoid broad or vague generalizations; give the necessary specifics of your message. Ultimately, after reading your letter (or even the introduction, for that matter), your recipient should know *why* you wrote the letter.

3. Simplicity

Simplicity will depend on your relationship with the recipient and your purpose for writing the letter. A short letter or e-mail to a friend should be fairly simple; going into elaborate detail or specifics will be superfluous. However, a business or professional letter should be relatively brief and direct, but still provide your reader with adequate information about who you are and why you are writing to him or her. Business people are often too busy to read through lengthy letters or e-mails, especially if they include unnecessary content. So, unless you're writing a letter that allows for extra creativity, such as an invitation, a note of congratulations, or a love letter, avoid ornate compositions and keep things simple. Your recipient will thank you!

4. Consistency

It is essential to be consistent throughout your letter; from format to formality, keep things uniform. The content of your letter should be consistent in terms of your ideas and information, as well as in the way that you present them through your tone and attitude. Again, a creative letter may call for something a little less traditional, but in keeping with the specific theme or type of your letter, you will want to maintain consistency to make the letter easier for you to write and for your recipient to read.

5. Personality

Your personality should shine through your letter, and the way you present yourself will determine how you will be perceived. Your self-projection (or the impression you give) will influence others' perceptions of you through your word choice, tone, and content. Your choice of words and the order in which you place them will reveal your tone and formality; this, in turn, will make up the content of your letter. Tone can be personal, impersonal, subtle, forceful, active, or passive. It can also be tactful, detailed, positive, formal, or informal. What kind of message do you want to send, and how do you want your attitude to be projected? This will speak volumes about your personality, professionalism, sincerity, and maturity. In writing your letter, you should show attention, interest, and a sense of action. Think about how you would present yourself in person and then translate this into your writing.

PART SIX: DIFFERENT KINDS OF LETTERS

From short congratulatory notes to professional cover letters, there is a letter for every occasion, situation, and sensation. In this section, we will consider and compare the most common kinds of letters. The examples that follow should give you a general idea of the kinds of letters you can write and the information that each one should include. The **purpose, tone,** and **structure** of each type of letter will be summarized. Following a description of each letter, you will see two short lists: **Five Words** and **Five Phrases**. These lists should get you thinking about the different kinds of words and phrases you can use when writing your own letters. Use these as a guide and be creative! Personalize your letters and write them in a way that genuinely reflects your character and emotions.

Acceptance Letter

Purpose: To formally accept an offer, most often a job offer. It reinforces professionalism and shows your new employer how much you appreciate his or her time and the opportunity that he or she has given you.

Tone: Passive, formal, positive, detailed

Structure: Start your acceptance letter by stating that you're accepting the offer. Then outline the details of the job (title, salary, benefits, schedule, flex time, and start date) to acknowledge that you agree with the employer's terms and conditions. This is especially important if any aspects of the original offer were unclear. Having the details in writing can help avoid future issues about any of the job's specifications (How Stuff Works 2013).

Some acceptance letters, rather than being written by you, come in the form of an offer letter from the employer. An offer letter will stipulate all the terms and conditions of employment and must be read, signed, and sent back to the employer immediately. Do this as soon as possible to confirm your acknowledgment and acceptance of the offer.

As a side note, if you communicated with someone from the company separately—such as an employee who referred you—you may want to send that person a short letter or e-mail of thanks for any part that he or she played in helping you get the position.

If you're writing the acceptance letter yourself (as opposed to simply signing and dating an offer from the employer), it should be short and to the point. Here, again, you will want to reiterate that you appreciate the career opportunity and that the employer chose the right candidate for the job.

Five Words: accept, affirm, delighted, glad, welcome

Five Phrases: agree to the terms, pleased to accept, I'm very enthusiastic, it really pleases me, I feel honored

Example: Acceptance Letter

Dear Mr. Brown:

Thank you so much for your call yesterday. I am pleased to accept your offer for the position of Advertising Manager and I am delighted at the opportunity.

To summarize our discussion, the key points we outlined were as follows:

- I will be responsible for managing the company's marketing communications program, including all advertising done on the company's web site.
- My salary will be $50,000 a year plus group benefits and a performance bonus after my one-year review.
- My immediate supervisor will be Angela Smith.
- I will have a private office and my own laptop and tablet for work purposes.

I am thrilled at the chance to be working with you and your team as of July 1. Thank you again for your offer and your confidence in my abilities. I am eager to be part of the team at MediaOne PR to increase its return on marketing and advertising investments.

Sincerely,

Brendan Abbott

Apology Letter

Purpose: To apologize to someone

Tone: Passive, tactful, personal, informal

Structure: Writing an apology letter is a fitting way to reflect on what you did or said that prompted you to write the letter in the first place. Putting your thoughts on paper will allow you to really examine the situation, explain yourself, and say what is on your mind.

In writing an apology, you will be communicating with someone you have wronged, so keep in mind how this person may be feeling when he or she receives your letter. The person may be sad, hurt, upset, or angry—so, it is crucial to be sincere in expressing regret, knowing that you may not get a response (or at least not right away).

Avoid beating around the bush or going off on a tangent. You made the mistake, so it is up to you to own up to it. Don't try to justify yourself or make excuses—**just say sorry**. Take the blame for your wrongdoing. You must always keep in mind *why* you are writing the letter, and doing so may even be easier for you than confronting the recipient face-to-face.

Recognize that you did something wrong and that you *can* make up for it. You may not be forgiven right away, but offering a genuine apology will show that you are truly repentant. Keep the letter simple and respectful, and admit that you were at fault. Let the recipient know that you sincerely want to make amends. The person may not get back to you soon, but your effort to make peace should at least ease the situation.

Five Words: accept, responsible, fault, admit, mistake

Five Phrases: I wish to apologize, I sincerely regret, I can offer no excuse, I cannot offer a viable explanation, I take responsibility

Example: Apology Letter

Dear Sarah:

I had the best intentions in mind when I made those comments about your short story reading last week. My suggestions were meant to help make you a better writer. You're extremely talented and I admire your writing ability; I didn't think my feedback would upset you.

I'm so sorry for what I said to you. I now know that I must think more carefully before I speak. My job is to teach, guide, and motivate you, and I let you down in failing to do so sensitively.

My sincerest apologies,

Hannah

Letter of Complaint

Purpose: To air your grievances. A letter of complaint will often be written to a person or company with whom you have had some sort of unsatisfactory experience. Did you purchase a product and are now unhappy with it? Did you receive bad service and you want to make a point of it? Although you are disgruntled or angry about the situation, you will want to maintain—at the very least—a neutral tone that formally conveys your frustration.

Tone: Tactful, detailed, forceful, impersonal

Structure: Before writing your letter, know your purpose and prepare all the information necessary to file your complaint. For example, you bought a product that is now faulty and you would like to return it. When and where did you buy it? Do you have any invoice numbers, receipts, or records of the product that would help the person you are writing to identify it? Do you know if the product is eligible for a refund or an exchange?

At the beginning of your letter, draw your recipient's attention to the matter you're going to address. For example, start your letter by writing, "I am writing to complain about . . ." or "I wish to express my dissatisfaction with . . . ." Keep it respectful, as you are writing to someone who has the power to either help you or ignore your complaint. Make sure you are clear and to the point about the problem. Do not leave any vital information out or any room for ambiguity.

Introduce your main argument as early as possible and state your reason for writing using a clear, strong voice. Once you have done this, you may want to explain further by adding background information or relevant details to your complaint.

Next, ask yourself what actions you expect the company to take. Be realistic and reasonable in your request, as you want the situation to be resolved as quickly and painlessly as possible.

If you need to include any documents to support your case, make sure you do so, as this will help expedite the process (Oxford Dictionaries 2013).

Avoid being negative. Despite your frustration, keep your tone calm and convey your feelings in a dignified way that gets your point across without sounding rude or angry.

Five Words: dissatisfied, experience, incident, resolve, error

Five Phrases: bring this matter to your attention, I would like to be reimbursed for, I've enjoyed being a client, was inconvenienced, please check your records

Example: Letter of Complaint

Vanessa Michaels

56 Cherry Hill Lane
Ottawa ON 36R 0P9
Daniel Black
Customer Service Manager
HS Home Care
Toronto ON 9LP 4B7

June 12, 2013

Dear Mr. Black:

I am writing to complain about the unsatisfactory service I received from your company on June 12, 2013, when I was visited at my home by a representative of HS Home Care, Mr. Fox.

Mr. Fox was two hours late for his appointment and offered no apology when he arrived at noon. He did not remove his muddy shoes upon entering my house, and consequently left a trail of dirt. Mr. Fox then proceeded to present a range of products to me that I had specifically told his assistant (by e-mail) I was not interested in. I repeatedly tried to ask Mr. Fox about the products that were of interest to me, but he refused to deal with my questions. We ended our meeting after 20 minutes without either of us having accomplished anything.

I am most upset that I wasted my morning (and half a day's vacation) waiting for Mr. Fox to show up. My impression of HS Home Care has been tarnished, and I am now concerned about how my existing business is being managed by your firm. Furthermore, Mr. Fox's failure to remove his muddy shoes has meant that I have had to use, and incur the expense of, a professional carpet cleaner. I am requesting a reimbursement of $140 for the carpet cleaning expense I incurred. Enclosed is a copy of the invoice.

I trust this is not the way HS Home Care wishes to conduct business with its customers. I have been with you since the company was founded and have never encountered such disrespectful treatment. Please send me a catalog or specification sheets of your patient home care items. I would welcome the opportunity to discuss matters further and to learn how you propose to prevent the recurrence of a similar situation. I look forward to hearing from you.

Sincerely,

Vanessa Michaels

Condolence Letter

Purpose: To express your sympathy for someone suffering from an unfortunate situation or loss (Lamb 2011)

Tone: Active, tactful, hopeful, personal, informal

Structure: Your letter should be brief, kind, and show how you can offer concrete help during this time of need. When writing to convey your condolences for a tragic event like a death, illness, financial loss, or divorce, it is best to write your letter by hand. Empathize with the recipient and think about the stages of grief—denial and isolation, anger, depression, acceptance, and healing—and how the person may be dealing with them. Adjust your message accordingly (Lamb 2011).

Be hopeful in your tone and avoid harsh or preachy words that could exacerbate the situation. To show your respect and sensitivity to the situation, consider the religious preferences and customs of the recipient when writing your letter. Indicate that you are there for the person (and the family, if they have also been affected) and offer suggestions as to how you can help. Let the recipient know that you are willing to provide assistance in any way possible.

End the letter on a warm note and consider sending your message with flowers or a small gift to show your sympathy. Be as comforting as possible, but make sure not to express pity for the person. Ensure that your message is timely and brief, and if you send a store-bought card, include your own note along with the one already inside. It may not seem like a grand gesture, but your thoughtfulness will be greatly appreciated and remembered.

Five Words: difficult, consolation, compassion, loss, concern

Five Phrases: a lovely person, extend my sympathies, saddened to learn, in this time of great sorrow, may your wonderful memories add comfort

Example: Condolence Letter

Dear Marnie,

Brent told me about Alex's passing. I'm so sorry. You have my sincerest condolences.

Alex was an amazing man; he was one of the smartest and most talented people I have ever known. I will never forget the time we threw him a surprise birthday party and invited all his university friends. He wasn't expecting anything that year because you had told him that you were going to a conference in New York. He was so surprised and excited—I'll never forget the look on his face when he saw his best friend, Chris, whom he hadn't seen for 10 years.

Alex will be missed by us all, but our memories of him will stay with us forever. He is at peace now, and we are better people for having known him. My thoughts are with you. Please let me know if you need any help with your kids during this time—I will be more than happy to help with anything you need.

Sincerely,

Katrina

Confirmation Letter

Purpose: To confirm details or agree to something in writing

Tone: Active, informal, detailed, impersonal

Structure: Confirmation letters are often short and to the point, so your writing should be simple. Confirmation letters or e-mails will be sent to verify appointments, travel arrangements, meetings, and events— essentially, time-specific tasks. For this reason, confirmation letters should be sent promptly.

In writing this type of letter, your main goal is to confirm dates, times, locations, and events. Make sure your recipient can validate these details and that you provide the proper contact information so that the person can reply to you as soon as possible. Provide specific facts to avoid confusion or ambiguity, and keep your letter brief and focused on the details: *who, what, where, when, why,* and *how.*

Five Words: accept, acknowledge, confirm, received, verify

Five Phrases: as agreed, I would like to confirm, I'm pleased to confirm, the changes indicate that, the agreement will now read

Example: Confirmation Letter

Dear Marissa:

I received your message and am happy to hear that John Barr has been booked for your June "Night of Novel Approaches" to present his Improving Communications workshop. To recap the details:

Date: Thursday, June 16, 2013

Time: 7:30 p.m.

Location: Rose Bookstore, Vancouver BC M9L 4W1

I understand that you'll be promoting the event through a press release, your Facebook page, your Twitter feed, and signs at the store. Please let me know if you need additional information from us to help with your promotions.

I'll call you next Monday to go over the details.

Regards,

Sophia

Letter of Congratulations

Purpose: To send well wishes. It should be short and simple, yet kind and positive.

Tone: Active, positive, personal, informal

Structure: Perhaps you have friends who just got engaged, a co-worker who recently had a baby, or a niece who just graduated from high school. In each of these situations, it would be appropriate to send a letter of congratulations. Just as you would verbally congratulate someone on an important milestone in his or her life, writing a personalized letter of congratulations is a simple yet effective way of expressing your happiness at someone's achievement or a joyful occasion.

As mentioned above, these types of letters are brief. Start your letter by congratulating the recipient on his or her accomplishment, whether that means buying a house, celebrating an anniversary, or landing a new job. Then state how happy you are for the person and give compliments or praise. Make him or her feel special! If you know the recipient well, add a comment that shows your close relationship for a warm, personalized touch.

Five Words: accomplishment, celebrate, exceptional, success, well-earned

Five Phrases: congratulate you on, recognize your accomplishment, offer warmest congratulations, wish you every happiness, what a wonderful achievement

Example: Letter of Congratulations

Dear Ryan,

Wow! You've done it again. Congratulations!

I just read in the *Seattle Star* that the story you wrote for Reader's Opinion just won a Gold Star Award for best promotion and that this is the second time you've won.

The client also gave you a fantastic mention in the article, noting that your DM packages for him have always been successes. Your track record is enviable and few copywriters have ever been able to achieve it.

You must feel great, and I'm sure your clients are more than impressed. This should bring you lots of new business in the coming year—not that you need it!

Great job, Ryan! I'm always amazed at how much I learn from you.

Sincerely,

Seth

Cover Letter

Purpose: To accompany your résumé when applying for a specific job. Its purpose is to elaborate on and highlight your main accomplishments while explaining how your skills and abilities make *you* the best candidate for the position.

Tone: Active, positive, enthusiastic, formal, detailed, impersonal

Structure: Since the point of writing a cover letter is to help you land a specific job, it is important to avoid language that is too formal, dry, or vague (Lamb 2011). The person reading your cover letter has undoubtedly already been through hundreds of other letters, so your goal is to capture his or her attention and make your letter stand out. Make the content of your letter as unique and interesting as possible to keep it from getting lost in the sea of letters in the employer's inbox. Cover letters must be kept to (less than) one page and are composed of around three paragraphs.

Introductory Paragraph (preceded by a greeting or salutation): A short paragraph stating why you are writing to the company (to apply for position X) and why you believe that your skills, abilities, and experiences make you an exceptional candidate for the job.

Body: A couple of paragraphs in which you highlight your previous positions and experiences that qualify you for position X. You must describe how these credentials will enable you to fulfill the company's (and the specific position's) requirements.

- If possible, use **keywords** from the job posting or advertisement to match your qualifications with those the company is seeking. As a reminder, always be **honest** in what those skills and abilities are; never communicate false information.

- Expand on the descriptions of specific positions or experiences from your résumé that highlight their relevance to position X.
- Tell the employer what makes *you* uniquely qualified for the position and project an impressive image without sounding arrogant or disrespectful.

Closing Paragraph (followed by a sign-off): A brief paragraph that summarizes the body of your letter and restates why your skill set makes you an excellent candidate for position X.

- Kindly tell the recipient (who will often be a hiring manager) the best ways to reach you (via telephone and/or e-mail), and be proactive in requesting further contact.
- Thank the employer for his or her time and consideration, and state that you are looking forward to hearing from him or her soon.

Most importantly, remember that every cover letter you write must be tailored **specifically** to the job for which you are applying. Although it takes extra time and effort to create a solid cover letter for each position, the quality of your finished product will be well worth it. You can be reassured that a thoroughly though out, well-written cover letter will make all the difference in helping you land your dream job.

Five Words: act(ed), streamline(d), coordinate(d), organize(d), demonstrate(d)

Five Phrases: reduced waste by 25 percent in six months, qualified the organization for accreditation, increased production by 15 percent, wrote an online training program, improved plant safety record

Example: Cover Letter

Jane Dixon
123 Spruce Avenue
Toronto ON M5J 2Y1

John Larsgaard, Human Resources Manager
AeroMed Pharmaceuticals
4562 Yonge Street
Toronto ON N7L 3P9

June 23, 2013

Re: Application for the Customer Service position

Dear Mr. Larsgaard:

Thank you for answering my questions earlier this week regarding your web site advertisement for the Customer Service position currently available at AeroMed Pharmaceuticals.

My qualifications match the responsibilities listed in your job posting. With over 10 years of customer service experience in increasingly challenging roles, I have advanced in my career through demonstrated initiative and the ability to work effectively under pressure. In my most recent position as Customer Support Representative at a large pharmaceutical manufacturing company, I had the opportunity to overhaul our entire department. My modifications increased our operations efficiency by 60 percent. I have developed the competence to operate independently in a complex environment, which has strengthened my communication and organizational skills. My education includes a secretarial diploma and courses in Organization and Human Resource Management. As stated in my résumé, I have an ongoing commitment to professional development. I would be available to start in this position immediately, with two weeks' notice to my current employer.

I look forward to hearing from you to further discuss this exciting opportunity. I can be reached at the number indicated below. A message can be left on my voicemail if I am not available. Thank you for your time and consideration.

Respectfully,

Jane Dixon
Cell: (555) 652-5945
Enclosure

Letter of Invitation

Purpose: To request someone's presence—a friend, a family member, a co-worker, or a colleague—at an event or function. These functions include weddings, birthday parties, graduations, religious ceremonies, house warming parties; the list is endless!

Tone: Positive, warm, active, personal, formal

Structure: Just as with letters of confirmation, it is important to pay attention to the specifics of an event or function. What is the occasion? When is it? Where is it? At what times will it start and end? Is there a dress code? Clearly outline the details of the event to ensure that your guests are aware of the *who, what, where, when, why*, and *how*. Keep it short, and let your writing convey your excitement and enthusiasm about the celebration. Give your guests multiple options to respond to your invitation as easily and efficiently as possible (e-mail; self-addressed, stamped RSVP card; telephone; online RSVP service, etc.).

Five Words: announce, celebrate, presence, welcome, company

Five Phrases: happy to announce, pleased to introduce, wish to invite, please join us, request your presence at

Example: Letter of Invitation

We invite you to share our joy and love as our daughter

Shoshana Leah

is called to the Torah as a Bat Mitzvah

February 12, 2014 at 10:30 a.m.

Congregation Shomrei Torah

Fair Lawn, NJ

Kiddush following services

Mr. and Mrs. Ethan Simms

RSVP

555-468-2141 simms93@email.com

Love Letter

Purpose: A love letter is one of the most enchanting types of correspondence you can write, as its purpose is to express love for another person. Writing a love letter is an exercise in self-discovery that allows you to look inward and reflect upon yourself, your significant other, and your relationship on a deeper level.

Tone: Positive, active, detailed, personal, informal

Structure: When writing a love letter, follow your heart and express your true feelings to your beloved. While revealing your emotions for this person, you will want to identify the traits you love so much about him or her: from her beauty or his handsomeness to his or her desirability, kindness, and commitment. You may wish to state how the person makes you feel (warm, loved, amazing, special, like you're the only one, etc.). You may also use quotes, metaphors, similes, or images from authors, poets, or artists to help carry your message of love.

Start the letter with a term of endearment. Go on to describe your shared memories, your sentiments about the person, and the little things about him or her that you find irresistible—reflecting and expanding on your thoughts about the person and how you feel when you're together.

You will want to stay away from stiff formality; after all, you are in love with this person and have shared many experiences with each other. Your goal is to make your letter sound as close to speech as possible, so feel free to use colloquialisms and contractions in your writing. You want your beloved to feel as though you are there, uttering your words and expressing your feelings in person.

As with other types of letters, take a break once you have finished writing so that you can review and edit the letter after some time has passed to distract yourself from its intensity. This will ensure that you say *what you want* in the *way that you intend it to be understood.*

You want your love letter to convey all the warmth and passion in your heart—for this reason, your love letter should be long and eloquent—it will probably be the longest of all the letters discussed in this book. You should not feel as though you need to hold anything back, but do not include anything that could reflect poorly on you if your letter were to be read by someone else.

Since the love letter is one of the more creative types of letters that you can write, stationery is an important medium for providing a personal touch and giving your letter a nice, unique appearance. This is essential, as the recipient will most likely want to keep the letter as a souvenir of you and your relationship.

Avoid impersonal forms of communication. As we all know, e-mails and other electronic media are impersonal by nature. For this reason, take the time and effort to show your loved one how much he or she means to you by *handwriting* your letter. This way, not only will you have the opportunity to be imaginative, but your physical letter will be a memento that can be kept and reread for years to come.

Five Words: admire, beautiful, passionate, memories, sweetest

Five Phrases: amazed by you, imagining us together, miss you, you are my, can't wait

Example: Love Letter

Sweetest Daria,

I miss you so much, my love! I think about you all the time. You are the first thing I think of when I wake up and the last thing on my mind before I go to sleep. I am so incredibly lucky to have found such an amazing woman. I miss you like crazy—it has been too long since the last time I saw you.

Your smile is so beautiful; whenever I think of your gorgeous face, my heart just melts. Whenever I see your smile or hear your voice, I forget about all the negativity in the world. You make me so happy, and I want to be with you all the time.

Daria, you are the most caring and selfless person I have ever met. You are patient, kind, and always there to support me 100 percent. The time you flew across the country to take care of my sick mother when I was away is just one of the ways your compassionate heart shines.

I always have a great time with you, no matter what we are doing or where we are. As long as you are by my side, even the most mundane activities become exciting. I hope that we'll see each other every day when I come back; I want to spend as much time with you as possible. I miss you so much, and I will love you forever.

Love always,

Jon

Offer Letter

Purpose: A legally binding letter communicating an offer and outlining the terms of employment

Tone: Active, direct, detailed, positive, formal

Structure: An offer letter is intended to offer the recipient a job. It clarifies expectations and specifies the details of employment: job title, salary, benefits, job responsibilities, flex time, dates and times, probationary period, travel requirements, vacation, promotions, variable compensation (such as bonuses, profit sharing, or commission), and any other relevant information, such as confidentiality or non-compete agreements. The offer letter should also explicitly state when you want it signed and returned, and specify any other documents that are required before employment starts. An offer letter answers the employee's questions and allows the employer to fulfill his or her duty to define the terms of employment.

An offer letter can propose either a fixed-term or an indefinite contract. In a fixed-term contract, the employment duration is set and the employee must agree to end the work relationship on a specific date— say, a year after the start date. From that point on, depending on the terms of employment, the employee's performance, and the company's needs, the employee may either receive an extension offer or comply with the original fixed term.

On the other hand, an indefinite contract has no set end date for the employee—the employee will continue working for the company until either he or she or the employer chooses to end the relationship. The employee may resign depending on his or her circumstances and job satisfaction, or the employer may choose to terminate the employee due to dishonesty, insubordination, or incompetence.

It is important for the recipient to sign and return the offer letter (in addition to any supporting documents) prior to the first day of work, as he or she must be familiar with the details and responsibilities of the job.

If possible, personalize your letter to help the employee feel welcome to the company. You can do this by stating how pleased you are to have the candidate join your company, or you could even send something along with the letter, like a welcome package or company merchandise. Think about what *you* would like to read (or perhaps have read) in an offer letter from an employer. What would make you feel welcome to a new company?

Avoid contractual implications or not clearly stating the terms of employment—there is no room for ambiguity here. According to Inc.com (2010), it is essential to make sure that your letter does not have phrases that imply indefinite employment or annual salary amounts (it is best to write these in hourly, weekly, or monthly terms, since an annual term implies employment for at least a year), as this will cause ambiguity.

It is a good idea to draft your offer letter first and have it reviewed by a lawyer to check that you are meeting all legal obligations in accordance with international labor standards. This will ensure the accuracy of your offer and avoid any misunderstandings between you and the recipient.

Five Words: accept, pleasure, unique, congratulate, welcome

Five Phrases: offer warmest congratulations, we are pleased to offer, delighted to have you join, it really pleases me, would like to welcome you

Example: Offer Letter

Mr. Roger Griffin
1532 SW Springlake Ct.
Portland, OR 12003

June 1, 2013

Dear Roger:

On behalf of BSB Group's Applied Technologies Branch, I am pleased to offer you the position of Sales Engineer, reporting to Eric Smith, Business Unit Manager, beginning on October 1. This position is to be compensated in the following manner:

- Your Base Rate is $6,800.00/month.
- You will participate in the BSB Sales Incentive Program.
- You will participate in the Applied Technologies Corporate Program.
- You are eligible to participate in the BSB Benefit Program as described in the literature provided to you.

This offer is contingent upon you satisfying the company's three-month probationary period and the education and reference verification requirements.

Please understand that this employment offer and any other BSB documents are in no way to be used as a contract of employment or any assurance of continued employment. Employment is at will and can be terminated at any time by either party. We look forward to welcoming you to BSB Group.

Sincerely,

Asher Fairfield
Assistant Manager, Regional Personnel

I accept the terms of employment and will start _____.

Signature _____

Date _____

Reference Letter

Purpose: To recommend someone for something (a job, an application to university, a volunteer position, etc.) and to testify to this person's skills, character, achievements, and ability to succeed. When possible, a recommendation letter can also provide examples of the quality of the candidate's work.

Tone: Active, tactful, positive, detailed, formal

Structure: A reference letter is written for someone with whom you have worked closely and whose skills and abilities you know well (a co-worker, a former student, an employee you have supervised, or even a friend or family member, depending on the situation)—someone you would be willing to give an extremely positive recommendation to.

Since the recommendation or reference letter is a formal document, even if the person is a close friend, remember that you are writing the letter to someone in a business or another type of organization. Thus, your tone should be honest, professional, and as formal as the organization to which you are writing.

References support applications and confirm a candidate's ability to exhibit the skills and abilities he or she described in his or her initial application. Therefore, it is important to know the candidate in a capacity that will allow you to write a valid and authentic reference.

Sometimes, a reference format or guideline is given by the employer or institution. It is important to follow the specifications to ensure that the letter is accepted and that the employer receives it in the required format.

Because the recipient of the letter does not know you personally, provide a brief background of who you are and your connection to the candidate. Confirm any facts you know about the candidate in relation to the positions he or she has held and the one that he or she is applying for. For example, if you worked with the person in the past, define his or her job title, role in the company, length of employment, and any special projects in which he or she excelled. Provide examples of the candidate's relevant skills, personal qualities, and qualifications for the job. Also make sure to list the individual's exceptional attributes. Did he or she participate in extracurricular activities or show leadership qualities? Stay positive and emphasize the individual's outstanding characteristics that make him or her stand out as the best candidate.

Close the letter on a personal note and reiterate the candidate's impressive credentials. Provide your contact information in case any additional facts about the candidate are required.

Avoid lying, writing in an informal tone, or stating any weaknesses. Although you are describing the candidate's positive qualities, never say anything false. Do not include any personal information about the applicant that is not relevant to the application, such as the candidate's race, political views, religion, nationality, marital status, age, or health.

Five Words: accept, delighted, commend, glad, welcome

Five Phrases: impressive performance, highly recommend, asset to any organization, valuable contribution, excellent team player

Example: Reference Letter (Job)

To Whom It May Concern:

Natalia Mekalanos was employed as an Administrative Assistant at TekMountain from 2002 to 2005. During her tenure with the company, Natalia was responsible for office support, including word processing, scheduling appointments, and creating newsletters and other office literature.

Natalia fulfilled her responsibilities with little supervision. The position required interaction with the public as well as the ability to liaise between different departments. Success in the job was dependent on strong communication and interpersonal skills.

I am happy to act as a reference for Natalia and can speak highly of her customer service skills, work ethic, computer literacy, and professionalism. Please feel free to contact me should you require further information.

Sincerely,

Benjamin Ciampi
Community Involvement Coordinator
TekMountain
(595) 355-1214
b.ciampi@tekmountain.net

Example: Reference Letter (College)

To Whom It May Concern:

I am pleased to recommend for your program Miriam Bell, who has been a student of mine in the mathematics department for the past three years. During that time, I have come to know her as a serious student and a role model for her peers.

Miriam is a rare type of student who combines exceptional natural ability with a willingness and eagerness to learn. Miriam is able to help her peers with difficult mathematical concepts, but she does so in a way that is both practical and non-condescending. Although she is aware of her innate talent in the area of mathematics, Miriam is constantly honing her skills. She is part of the school's Mathletics Team, which challenges local university students in mathematical competitions. She is also active in the school community as a cheerleader and a member of Books for Change while playing defense on our school's soccer team.

Miriam would make an excellent candidate for early admissions. I recommend her without hesitation. Should you have any questions, please feel free to contact me.

Sincerely,

Simone Smith
Head of Mathematics
Chicago Institute of Higher Education
(916) 553-8752
s.smith@chicagoinstitute.edu

Rejection Letter

Purpose: To decline a job offer, an offer from a university, or any other situation that would require you to politely refuse or reject something. Writing a rejection letter is less confrontational than refusing or rejecting something in person and is a suitable way of ensuring that you deal with the matter directly.

Tone: Active, tactful, detailed, formal

Structure: As with many of the other types of letters we have discussed, rejection or refusal letters should also be succinct. Keep your letter brief and straight to the point. Be clear, direct, and confident in your tone and content.

Thank the recipient for his or her time and any offers or opportunities that he or she has given you. Refusing something does not mean being brusque about it; graciously and kindly decline the offer or request, and realize that you may still need him or her (or vice versa!) in the future. Don't burn any bridges! If you wanted to accept the recipient's offer or grant his or her request, but were unable to do so, make sure to include the reasons why in your letter, as this will help the recipient understand why you have made the decision to decline.

Five Words: decision, decline, encourage, regret, re-apply

Five Phrases: after careful consideration, thank you for applying, not able at this time, doesn't qualify, our application period is closed

Example: Rejection Letter

James Brandenberg
Human Resources Manager
752 Meadowgreen Avenue
Seattle, WA 11245

June 22, 2013

Natalia Mekalanos
65 Starcrest Lane
Seattle, WA 11145
natalia.mekalanos@email.com

Dear Ms. Mekalanos:

I want to thank you for your interest in the RPN position at Seattle General Hospital and for all the time you put into the interview process. Unfortunately, we will not be offering the position to you. While your education qualifications are very impressive, we have chosen a candidate who has more hands-on experience. However, we will keep your résumé on file and if any other jobs become available, we will keep you in mind. After you have gained some experience through volunteering or in another position in the field, we hope that you will re-apply to Seattle General Hospital.

On behalf of Seattle General Hospital, thank you for your time, interest, and effort, and I wish you the best in your future career.

If you have any questions, please do not hesitate to contact me at (646) 773-5190.

Sincerely,

James Brandenberg
Human Resources Manager

Letter of Request

Purpose: To ask the recipient to do something that he or she may or may not want (or have) to do

Tone: Passive, tactful, detailed, positive

Structure: You may need to be more persuasive in writing a letter of request compared to other types of letters, especially if you know that the recipient is not particularly keen on fulfilling the request.

The benefit of writing such a letter is that it allows the recipient to think the request over without the pressure of your physical presence. It is important to be friendly and polite when writing such a letter; your recipient should feel as though his or her skills and abilities are imperative to accommodating your request. Ask courteously and do not be demanding. Show the recipient what's in it for him or her and state exactly what you would like him or her to do and when to get back to you.

Focus on the details of your request and, once again, keep it brief. Make it easy for the recipient to answer you promptly and positively. Be gracious and friendly in your tone and thank the reader in advance for anything he or she can do to help you or answer your questions.

Five Words: ask, appreciate, request, inquire, respond

Five Phrases: ask for your assistance, as soon as possible, I'm writing to inquire, would you be willing to supply, I need your help in locating

Example: Letter of Request

Ms. Jessica Lam, CAE, CMP
Executive Director
CFED Education Foundation
Senior Vice President, Education
CFED
1200 Aberdeen Street, Suite 200
Los Angeles, CA 88003

September 1, 2013

Dear Jessica:

I'm the author of *Meetings and Events*, a book I hope you'll consider for possible inclusion in your catalog.

Meetings and Events provides a number of up-to-date ideas and resources to help plan quick, budget-friendly meetings and industry events.

This book will be an excellent fit with your current offerings, especially for people new to the education industry. Using simple language, it explains the details involved in planning successful events and provides lots of real-life examples. Industry veterans can use the book as a resource for finding vendors as well as definitive "best sources."

I have enclosed a copy for your review. *Meetings and Events* is published by Education Press (New York, NY; February 2013) and retails for $22.00. I've included a few recent book reviews as well as a brief biography.

I look forward to working together to add this book to your catalog.

Regards,

Mira Torres, CMP

Resignation Letter

Purpose: To resign from something (in most cases, a job)

Tone: Passive, tactful, formal, personal

Structure: Regardless of your reason for wanting or needing to leave, it is important to tell your employer in a diplomatic manner that you will be resigning from the company, without burning any bridges along the way. In essence, you want to keep your personal relationships intact when leaving, without ruining your reputation for the future.

Your aim in writing a resignation letter is to assure your boss that he or she is not to blame for your departure. Even if you are leaving because you are unhappy or dissatisfied with your job or your boss, you do not want to convey any negative emotions through your writing. Remember that this is a professional letter and should be treated as such. It is not a complaint and should not be written as one, although you may have some unresolved issues that still need to be dealt with.

Thank your employer for the job opportunity and clearly state your reasons for leaving in a diplomatic and formal tone. You may not need to go into full detail, but you should tie up any loose ends and explain how any pending work will be finished or turned over to other employees. Don't leave your employer hanging.

Leave an ample amount of time between your notice of resignation and last day at the company. This will allow you to finish up any ongoing projects or to delegate any work that you were supposed to complete. Leaving this buffer of time will also give your employer a chance to start searching for a replacement, if necessary.

In closing your letter, thank the employer for your time with the company and mention how much you appreciate his or her understanding of the situation.

After handing over your letter, it is best to follow up with a face-to-face meeting to further discuss the details of your resignation.

Five Words: appreciate, built, enjoyed, opportunity, valuable (invaluable)

Five Phrases: continue to be challenged in new ways, provided a growth opportunity, gained valuable skills, excellent learning experience, move in a new direction

Example: Resignation Letter

To: Ray Ramsay, SD Department Manager

I am pleased to announce that I have accepted a position with GenTech Corporation's Development and Testing Unit effective March 18, 2013. My last day in the Systems Development Department will be March 12, 2013.

I have thoroughly enjoyed working with you during my four-and-a-half years in the department, and it is with some regret that I move forward. However, I believe that this is a positive change that will provide new challenges and opportunities for my career.

Working with the SD Department has allowed me to gain a great deal of experience. I would like to take this opportunity to thank you for everything you have done to make my time at AlphaSolutions so rewarding. I also wish you every success in your future endeavors.

I welcome the possibility of working with you again in the future.

Kindest regards,

Kyle

Termination Letter

Purpose: To terminate an employee. (Note: Most companies have their own policies or guidelines as to how termination letters should be written, so you may want to consult your company's policies before drafting your termination letter.) Since you are the one terminating the employee, be fair in ensuring that you have addressed your concerns with regard to the situation.

Tone: Formal, detailed, passive, tactful

Structure: The termination letter should be both formal and professional, regardless of the employee's type of job. Although you may have been close to the person being terminated, it is vital to keep your personal relationship separate from your professional one. The letter should be printed on company stationery and either given to the employee directly (in a private meeting) or mailed. It should indicate whether the employee is being terminated with or without cause.

Terminating an employee *with cause* means that he or she was either dishonest (committed theft or fraud), insubordinate (broke company policies), or incompetent (unable to perform the job appropriately). Terminating someone with cause typically means that he or she will not be given a severance package. The reason(s) for terminating the employee must be described in sufficient detail so as not to breach any legal terms or obligations.

Terminating an employee *without cause* means that the employee is being terminated due to reasons beyond the employer's control. In this case, a severance package will be offered to the employee. Note that as an employer, you have an ethical and moral obligation to explain to your employee why you are letting him or her go.

In either case, when writing your termination letter, consult international labor standards (for your country), as they set the rights and responsibilities that both employers and employees must follow.

After stating the reason for termination, explain the next steps and what the employee can expect at this point. This includes discussing things like severance pay, final pay, additional compensation, etc. Although the letter may be the first notification of the employee's termination, give him or her the chance to discuss the details of the letter in person.

Regardless of the reason, termination should not violate human rights or employment standards. There must also be a termination policy in place that states your company's responsibilities. According to hrcouncil.ca (2013), the termination letter should state the effective date of termination and any payment or compensation that the employee is being offered.

Remember, just as with the offer letter, your termination letter should be reviewed by or written with a lawyer to ensure that it meets legal standards and is non-discriminatory. The employee still has the right to seek legal counsel if he or she so chooses, so be detailed and careful in your wording.

If the termination is to take effect immediately (rather than, say, in two weeks to a month), the employment standards allow the employer to pay the employee in lieu of a working notice period.

If the employee is being terminated without cause, show sympathy, focus on his or her strengths, and offer any possible assistance in helping him or her find a job, such as providing a reference letter. In any case, review the letter with the employee to ensure that he or she understands its terms, in addition to his or her rights as an employee.

Conclude your letter by restating the details of the termination and the next steps that should (or will) be taken by both the employer and the employee being terminated.

Five Words: decision, end, terminate, regret, final

Five Phrases: with full consideration, I regret to inform you, effective immediately, terminate your employment, have made the decision

Example: Termination Letter

Kayla Cooper
Senior Acquisitions Manager
Worther Book Co.
420 Paper Street
New York, NY 10003

July 5, 2013

James Henderson
65 Pine Street
Brooklyn, NY 19998

Dear Mr. Henderson:

I regret to inform you that your position with Worther Book Co. will be terminated for cause, effective immediately. Your employment, as discussed during the termination meeting, is being terminated because you committed company resources to a competitor after I informed you that the company would not provide these resources nor seek a relationship with that competitor.

Your actions were in violation of our company policy and our code of conduct.

You will receive your final paycheck on Friday, our regular pay day, and it can either be mailed to your home address, or you can make an appointment with your supervisor to pick it up.

The enclosed benefits status letter outlines the status of your benefits upon termination and all other information regarding your severance package. We received from you your office keys and the company owned cell phone at the termination meeting.

Please keep the company informed of your contact information so that we may provide information that you may need from us in the future, such as your W-2 form.

If I can be of any help during this transition, please do not hesitate to contact me directly.

Sincerely,

Kayla Cooper
Senior Acquisitions Manager

Thank You Letter

Purpose: To show your gratitude to someone

Tone: Active, positive, personal, enthusiastic

Structure: Although thank you letters may seem to be rarer than the other types of letters included in this book, by no means does this discredit their importance.

The extra time and effort it takes to handwrite a thank you card, note, or letter will show the recipient just how much you appreciate what he or she has done for you. Thank you letters should be sent shortly after an event (interview, wedding, etc.) and can help maintain and even strengthen your relationships with others.

It is important for your thank you letter to be genuine and enthusiastic. You are expressing your gratitude, after all, so you want to show this through your tone and choice of words.

You may also want to get creative with your letter—perhaps write it on eye-catching stationery or on a unique card—for that personalized touch of sincerity.

Five Words: enjoyed, kindness, touched, unforgettable, surprise

Five Phrases: more than kind, warm hospitality, generous gift, I will always be thankful for, thrilled to receive

Example: Thank You Letter (Post-Interview Follow Up)

Max Badgley
1422 Ocean Pacific Drive
Los Angeles, CA 678910

July 21, 2013

Dr. Roizenfield
Lead Scientist
Rats and Pumpkins Field Research Team
13 Rodentia Drive
Orange Patch, CA 131313

Dear Dr. Roizenfield,

I would like to thank you for taking the time to interview me for the position of Assistant Field Researcher on the Rats and Pumpkins Field Research Team. I know how busy your schedule is, and I greatly appreciate the time you cleared for the interview yesterday afternoon.

Making the trip down to Orange Patch and seeing the team in action has only boosted my desire to contribute to this wonderful project. The ecological interaction between rats and pumpkins is of considerable importance, and anything I can do to contribute to the team's research in this area will be time well spent, not to mention a personal blessing.

I am particularly interested in the night shift and the nocturnal symbiosis between rats and pumpkins; I am thrilled to research such a striking phenomenon, and I'm not afraid of the long hours! I have always been a night owl—or a night rat, if you permit me the expression—and a chance to pursue this significant study would be a great opportunity, both personally and professionally.

I am looking forward to hearing from you in the next two weeks, as you indicated. The potential of this opportunity is truly exciting, and I greatly appreciate your time and interest.

Yours sincerely,

Max Badgley

PART SEVEN: REFINING YOUR LETTER

Congratulations! You have now finished writing your letter. The only thing left is to edit, revise, and polish it. Depending on the type and length of your letter, this process may not take very long at all. However, even if the editing process is quick, you still want to send a letter that is error-free and conveys your tone, thoughts, emotions, and information clearly and effectively.

When writing a personal letter or correspondence of high importance or priority, it is best to take some time—a day or so—between writing and revising it. Re-reading the letter with fresh eyes will allow you to spot any discrepancies between what you have written and what you actually mean to say. It will also ensure that your tone is appropriate and that you include any information you may have missed the first time. You may even want to enlist a friend (or a professional editing service like Scribendi.com) to help you with the editing process.

Revision and polishing

When revising and polishing your letter, you will want to edit and proofread for the following.

Content: The content of your letter comprises its main message and conveys the purpose for writing it. Your content is the information that gives your letter value and meaning, and it will be best brought out with proper style, form, word choice, word order, format, spelling, grammar, and punctuation. Your content should be correct, complete, and audience-appropriate.

Style: Style is not so much about *what* you say as *how* you say it; it is the mode and form by which you express your thoughts, and includes tone and voice. Are your sentences simple and direct, or are they long and elaborate? Have you chosen the proper words to convey your message meaningfully? Does your voice shine through your formality and tone? These are the questions you should ask yourself when you consider the style of your writing. Your style will come through your writing the more you practice. In developing your own style, your goal is to create a piece of writing that is coherent, graceful, and accomplishes your purpose through your choice of words.

Tone: As mentioned earlier, tone refers to your written expressiveness and is dictated by your audience and purpose. It is this manner or expressiveness that allows you to convey your emotions. Generally, to set the tone of your writing, write how you would like to read. Remember, you want your tone to reflect your purpose and the audience.

Voice: Voice refers to the style and personality of your writing. Just as the spoken word conveys your tone and character, your voice in a piece of writing aims to do the same. Although you intend to keep your voice true to yourself, you also want it to agree with the occasion, purpose, and audience.

Form: Form is classified according to the purpose and the type of letter you are writing. There are three main forms of writing: expository, persuasive, and personal. In expository writing, your main goal is to provide information or explain something. In persuasive writing, your objective is to convince your reader of your ideas or beliefs. In personal writing, your aim is to share with your reader your ideas and experiences, giving you the chance to be both creative and expressive.

The form of your letter should correlate with the specific type of letter you are writing.

Concision: Concision refers to how brief your writing is. Being concise is important because you don't want to waste your reader's time with superfluous information or unnecessary wordiness. Again, how succinct you are depends on the type of letter and your purpose for writing it. Some types of letters, like thank you notes, typically demand that you be short, sweet, and to the point. Other types of letters, like love letters, are more extensive. In general, keep brevity in mind as you write, and limit your letter to a length that is suitable for its type and the recipient.

Word Choice: Word choice refers to the terms you use to describe your thoughts and feelings and transmit your information. Do your words convey your meaning appropriately? Do they reflect your thoughts accurately? Are they too technical or too simplistic for the type of letter you are writing? Here are some tips:

- Avoid contractions in formal documents.
- Make sure the recipient is familiar with technical terms/jargon.
- Start a sentence or paragraph with "Second" only when there's a "First" in a preceding sentence or paragraph.
- Avoid using a word in its own definition.
- Use words in the appropriate context.
- Use the right words, prepositions, and other parts of speech.
- Use the correct forms of words (e.g., don't use "drive" when it should be "driving").

Word Order: Word order refers to how you place your words. Do your words appear in the *correct* order? Does their sequence let your sentences and paragraphs flow smoothly, making your letter easy to read and understand? Have you mixed up the order of words anywhere?

- Make sure that what a word or phrase is referring to is clear (e.g., "this" or "that").

- Identify what a phrase is being compared to (e.g., "it goes slower"—slower than what?).
- Place adverbs close to the verbs they modify.

Format: The format of a letter refers to how the letter is laid out. Letters typically begin with a greeting, explain their purpose in the introduction, develop their content in the body, summarize their main points in the conclusion, and close with a sign-off. The format may be more or less formal, or contain more or less information, depending on the type of letter you are writing. For example:

Greeting: Dear Julie,

Introduction: I am writing to congratulate you on . . .

Body: (A few paragraphs about why you are congratulating Julie)

Conclusion: Congratulations again on your accomplishment . . .

Sign-off: Kind regards, (followed by your name)

Format also refers to the medium and method by which you will be writing and sending your letter. Are you handwriting or typing it? Will you be sending it in the mail or electronically via e-mail?

Spelling: Spelling refers to the formation of your words. Are your words spelled and capitalized correctly? Are they punctuated properly? Have you carefully checked for homonyms (words that sound the same, but are spelled differently) to ensure that you convey your intended meaning? Again, ask yourself these questions while writing your letter *and* while revising it. If you are writing your letter electronically, use a spell checker to uncover any errors that you may have missed. A spelling and grammar check won't typically catch all your mistakes (such as using the wrong word), but it will make a dramatic difference to the overall accuracy of your letter.

Grammar: Grammar pertains to the structural rules of your letter. Are you using the proper nouns, pronouns, verbs, adjectives, adverbs, tenses, and sentence types? Do all of these elements come together to create a coherent letter that flows smoothly and gets your message across effortlessly? Look for errors in the following:

- Capitalization
- Comma splices
- Correlative conjunctions ("Either . . . or"; "Not only . . . but also")
- Missing words
- Missing/extra article(s)
- Using symbols (e.g., "&") instead of full words (e.g., "and") in sentences
- Run-on sentences (sentences that are too long)
- Sentence fragments (sentences that cannot stand on their own because they fail to contain at least one independent clause)
- Number categories (singular/plural)
- Starting a sentence with a numeral (e.g., "49 horror-stricken onlookers . . .")
- Subject/verb agreement
- "Who"/"that" confusion
- Verb tenses

Punctuation: Punctuation marks help convey your tone and get your expression across in the way you intend. Have you used commas, periods, apostrophes, hyphens, exclamation marks, quotation marks, and question marks appropriately?

Always keep your audience in mind—for *whom* are you writing? Considering this while writing your letter will allow you to focus your content *and* enable your ideas to flourish and flow smoothly.

Be particular when it comes to your motivation for writing the letter and the message that you wish to send. Since you want to convey your thoughts and emotions just as clearly as you want them to be understood, it is important to use proper language and to cover the **five Ws and one H** (*who, what, where, when, why*, and *how*) in the outline of your letter.

After developing your outline, complete any additional research necessary to fill in the gaps. You may require further information about the recipient or a certain circumstance or situation. For example, you may need more facts about a candidate before you can write a strong letter of recommendation for the person. Or, if you are writing a complaint about a malfunctioning product, you may need more details about it from receipts or invoices.

Write or type the first draft of your letter double-spaced to make it easier for you to see mistakes and insert revisions. It is also a smart idea to use a dictionary or thesaurus when writing and revising your letter because it will give you the opportunity to be creative and expand your vocabulary.

Since writing is, in essence, the creation of meaning and information, it is considered an art form. In producing your letters, you are encouraged to be creative and to let your personality shine. This can be accomplished through your word choice and writing style as well as through the physical attributes of your letter—font (size, color, and type), format, stationery, attachments, and envelopes. Think outside the box and use this letter-writing opportunity to create something unique!

A final note

Letters, (post)cards, notes, e-mails, and, to a greater extent, memos and faxes, are sent as personal correspondences to friends, family members, acquaintances, and co-workers (Bly 2004). Letters have traditionally been the most formal of the bunch and, as such, should be written with the purpose of conveying personal or sensitive information intended for a single person (or just a few people; think family members). In general, unless you are writing on behalf of a professional or academic organization, letters are not required to be as rigidly formatted as other types of documents.

Therefore, there are only a few general guidelines to remember when writing your letter. If you are writing it by hand, make your penmanship clear and legible. Most people today choose *not* to write letters by hand, as this method has quickly become outdated with the rise of technology, so it is nice to receive a handwritten letter that has clearly taken time, effort, and creativity.

If you are typing your letter on a computer or another electronic device, keep your font reasonably sized (anywhere from 8 to 12 points, similar to the typical size of handwriting), and use a clear font for easy reading. Use **bold**, *italics*, <u>underline</u>, color, punctuation, or capitalization for emphasis. You can even use a combination of these formatting tools to create your desired effect. (Note: Do so consistently and moderately, as applying too many stylistic elements—which can easily be subject to overuse—results in a cluttered, over-the-top appearance. Avoid capitalizing *too* much, or it will look like you are YELLING.) Don't hesitate to get creative if the occasion calls for it—this is part of the fun of letter writing! So, while keeping in mind a general format or template to work from, make the letter your own. After all, *your* thoughts, ideas, and emotions are being crafted into a unique and tangible piece of communication, so why not make your letter stand out?

CONCLUSION

As with other forms of writing, letter writing will improve the way you communicate with others and strengthen your relationships, new or old. This is exactly what this book has taught you: how to write effective, winning letters that will achieve their desired aims while keeping this art form alive.

We have covered the mediums and methods of letter writing; digital communication and professionalism; preparing, planning, and structuring your letter; different kinds of letters; and refining your letter through editing and proofreading. All these topics are meant to help you create purposeful, convincing letters and reach your goals by enhancing your communication skills. The most effectual letters are brief, simple, specific, consistent, and show your personality. By following the guidelines outlined in this book, your letters are sure to be a success.

Since various occasions call for different types of letters, there will be plenty of opportunities to hone your (letter-) writing abilities and engage in this vanishing craft. Use this book (and the resources on Scribendi.com) to help you compose your next letter—whether it is an invitation, an acceptance letter, or a cover letter—and see where the results take you. The joy and excitement of receiving a letter—especially one that has been written by hand—is unparalleled, and the time and effort you put into writing your letter will speak volumes about your character. So, what are you waiting for? Grab a pen and a piece of paper (or your cell phone, laptop, or tablet), and start writing a letter today!

BONUS: TIPS ON WORDS AND PHRASES

Avoiding clichés

Clichés are overused, often outdated, words and phrases that are no longer effective at getting their meaning across. Avoid using clichés, especially in formal documents, as they give the impression of laziness and can (almost) always be replaced with more contemporary language.

Clichés to avoid:

agree to disagree

almighty dollar

among those present

ancestor

break the news gently

breakneck speed

but that's another story

by leaps and bounds

commercial pursuits

down through the ages

each and every one

every walk of life

fast and furious

goes without saying

gone but not forgotten

in any way, shape, or form

last but not least

nipped in the bud

no sooner said than done

powers that be

ripe old age

skeleton in the closet

words fail me

Commonly mixed-up words and their meanings

Similar sounding words (or homophones) are easy to mix up and are often missed by spell check. Take the time to review these commonly mixed-up words (along with their meanings) to avoid accidentally using the wrong word.

Commonly mixed-up words and their meanings:

Words — Meanings

accept — to receive

except — to exclude

advise — to counsel (verb)

advice — counsel (noun)

affect — to influence or change

effect — a result (noun); to bring about (verb)

coarse — rough

course — a direction of progress

counsel — advice (noun); to advise (verb)

council — a group or an assembly

decent — proper or respectable

descent — act of descending (noun)

descend — to come down (verb)

dissent — disagreement (noun); to disagree (verb)

enforce — to force

in force — in power, in effect

elicit — to draw out

illicit — illegal, improper

farther — in space

further — in thought

loose — unattached, free

lose — to suffer loss

precede — to go before

proceed — to begin, to continue

they're — they are

their — possessive pronoun

there — adverb indicating a place

Keeping it concise

Brevity is important, especially when it comes to letter writing. Keep your letters concise by using shorter and simpler words and phrases to get your ideas across.

Words that can be made more concise:

Instead of: — Use:

abbreviate — shorten

antithesis — opposite

ascertain — find out

autonomous — independent

concept — idea

currently — now

deficit — shortage

demonstrate — show

duplicate — copy

elucidate — clarify

facilitate — ease, simplify, help

feasible — possible

homogeneous — similar

inundate — flood

obtain — get

optimum — best

potentially — possibly, likely

subsequent — next

sufficient — enough

terminate — end

viable — workable

Phrases that can be made more concise:

Instead of: — Use:

a large number of — many

along the lines — like

as a general rule — generally

at all times — always

at your earliest convenience — now, soon

by means of — by

despite the fact — although

exhibits the ability — can

has proven itself to be — has proved, is

hold a meeting — meet

inasmuch as — since

in many cases — often

in order to — to

in the event that — if

in the majority of instances — usually, generally

in the near future — soon

it is clear that — clearly

on a daily basis — daily, every day

on the basis of — by, from

prior to that time — before

start off — start

subsequent to — after

take action — act

the reason why is that — because

with reference to — about

with the result that — so that

Avoiding redundancies

Redundant words and phrases are those that are unnecessary to the meaning of a sentence. They add information that is already available through the sentence's inherent structure and are therefore nonessential and excessive. Avoid redundancies in your letters and all other written documents.

Redundancies and their substitutions:

Redundancy — Substitution

absolutely essential — essential

actual experience — experience

adding together — adding

an honor and a privilege — an honor

any and all — any

basic essentials — essentials

by means of — by

continue on — continue

current status — status

different varieties — varieties

final outcome — outcome

first and foremost — first

first priority — priority

goals and objectives — goals

honest truth — truth

joined together — joined

mixed together — mixed

mutual cooperation — cooperation

one and the same — the same

personal opinion — opinion

point in time — time

reason why — why

refer back to — refer to

true facts — facts

whether or not — whether

you may or may not know — you may know

Spelling words correctly

The words in the list below are often misspelled. Please review these words (which are spelled in American English) in order to spell them correctly in your letters and other written documents.

Commonly misspelled words:

accidentally

accommodate

acknowledgment

bargain

beginning

benefited

canceled

committee

disappoint

embarrass

February

guarantee

immediately

judgment

manageability

noticeable

occurred

privilege

questionnaire

receive

renown

separate

supersede

unnecessary

until

Wednesday

Using modern phrases

Using antiquated words or phrases makes your writing appear outdated and will often be looked upon negatively. Instead of using such phrases, use language that is more natural and contemporary.

Old-fashioned phrases and their modern counterparts:

Instead of: — Use:

kindly — please

advise us — let us know

this will acknowledge your — as you requested

endeavor — try

in view of the fact — because

in lieu of — instead of

we deem it advisable — we suggest

state — say

in compliance with your request — as you requested

at the present time — now

in the event that — if

in the near future — soon

similar to — like

Acknowledgments and Works Cited

All references within this text are fully acknowledged and, where possible, linked directly to the source material. We offer two alphabetical lists of all references and works cited within this guide. The first list consists of online resources and the second refers to those in print.

Online references
About.com

Follow-Up Letter Sample

http://jobsearch.about.com/od/morejobletters/a/followupletter.htm

Thank You Letters

http://jobsearch.about.com/od/thankyouletters/a/thankyouletters.htm

Ben Locker & Associates – The Copywriting Agency

Writing Good Apology Letters

http://www.benlocker.co.uk/how-to-write-a-good-apology-letter/

Daily Writing Tips

Writing a Reference Letter

http://www.dailywritingtips.com/writing-a-reference-letter-with-examples/

eHow Money

Proper Office Etiquette for Writing Letters

http://www.ehow.com/info_8415301_proper-office-etiquette-writing-letters.html

How Stuff Works

How to Write an Acceptance Letter for a New Job

http://money.howstuffworks.com/business/getting-a-job/how-to-write-job-acceptance-letter.html

How to Write a Letter.net

How to Write a Confirmation Letter

 http://www.howtowritealetter.net/How-To-Write-a-Confirmation-Letter.html

How to Write a Request Letter

http://www.howtowritealetter.net/How-To-Write-a-Request-Letter.html

How to Write Congratulation Letters

http://www.howtowritealetter.net/How-To-Write-Congratulation-Letters.html

How to Write Thank You Letters

http://www.howtowritealetter.net/How-to-Write-Thank-You-Letters.html

hrcouncil.ca

Keeping the Right People

http://hrcouncil.ca/hr-toolkit/keeping-people-termination.cfm

Inc.com

How to Write a Termination Notice

http://www.inc.com/guides/2010/04/termination-letter.html

How to Write an Offer Letter

http://www.inc.com/guides/how-to-write-an-offer-letter.html

JobSeekersAdvice.com

Resignation Letter—How to Write a Resignation Letter

http://jobseekersadvice.com/employment-issues/resignation-letter-how-to-write-a-resignation-letter/

Library Online

Structuring Letters

http://www.libraryonline.com/default.asp?pID=46

Merriam-Webster

Letter

http://www.merriam-webster.com/dictionary/letter

Monster.ca

Writing a Good Cover Letter (Or How Not to Write a Cover Letter)

http://career-advice.monster.ca/resumes-cover-letters/cover-letter-tips/how-not-to-write-a-cover-letter-canada/article.aspx

Ontario Ministry of Labour

Employment Standards

http://www.labour.gov.on.ca/english/es/

Oxford Dictionaries

Letters of Complaint

http://oxforddictionaries.com/words/letters-of-complaint

Plain Language.gov

Writing Effective Letters

http://www.plainlanguage.gov/howto/guidelines/letters.cfm

Power to Change

How to Write a Love Letter

http://powertochange.com/sex-love/howtoloveletter/

Preserve Articles

How to Write Invitation Letters on Different Functions and Ceremonies

http://www.preservearticles.com/201105036196/how-to-write-invitation-letters-on-different-functions-and-ceremonies.html \

Scribendi.com

How to Write a Candidate Rejection Letter

http://www.scribendi.com/advice/how_to_write_a_candidate_rejection_letter.en.html

How to Write a Formal Letter

http://www.scribendi.com/advice/how_to_write_a_formal_letter.en.html

The Daily Beast

The Good Word

http://www.thedailybeast.com/newsweek/2009/01/17/the-good-word.html

The Telegraph

Top 5 Rules for Writing Love Letters

http://www.telegraph.co.uk/culture/books/9075220/Top-5-rules-for-writing-love-letters.html

WikiHow

How to Write a Love Letter

http://www.wikihow.com/Write-a-Love-Letter

<u>**Print references**</u>

Bly, Robert W. *Webster's New World Letter Writing Handbook.* Indianapolis, IN: Wiley, 2004.

Lamb, Sandra E. *How to Write It: A Complete Guide to Everything You'll Ever Write.* New York, NY: Ten Speed Press, 2011.

Maggio, Rosalie. *How to Say It: Choice Words, Phrases, Sentences, and Paragraphs for Every Situation.* Paramus, NJ: Prentice-Hall, 1990.

Stewart, Kay L., and Kowler, Marian E. *Forms of Writing: A Brief Guide and Handbook.* Scarborough, ON: Prentice-Hall, 1991.

Connect with Scribendi.com online:

Contact Scribendi.com: http://www.scribendi.com/contact

Twitter: http://twitter.com/Scribendi_Inc

Facebook: http://www.facebook.com/ScribendiInc

Scribendi.com's bookstore: http://www.scribendi.com/bookstore

Scribendi.com's blog: http://www.scribendi.com/advice/

ABOUT THE AUTHOR

Scribendi.com was founded in 1997 as one of the world's first online editing and proofreading companies. Based in Ontario, Canada, the company's primary goal is to provide clients with fast, reliable, and affordable revision services. Today, Scribendi.com is the world's largest online proofreading and editing company.

Made in the USA
San Bernardino, CA
28 May 2017